STO

FAVORITE books

Young Adults' Choices 1993-1995

INTERNATIONAL
Reading Association

800 Barksdale Road, PO Box 8139
Newark, Delaware 19714-8139, USA

YOUNG • ADULTS' • CHOICES

Logo illustration by Natalie Nelson

Each year since 1987 publishers have sent 100 to 200 new books for young adults to each of several test sites across the United States. At these sites teenagers read and evaluate the books and vote for their favorites; some 4,000 ballots are cast annually. The books with the most votes—about 30 each year—are selected as Young Adults' Choices. The test site team leaders and members of the IRA committee that administers the project prepare descriptions of the winners. The annotated list is published in the November issue of the *Journal of Adolescent & Adult Literacy* and is reproduced and widely circulated as a separate brochure.

The production of the Young Adults' Choices lists that appear in this book involved several years of work by IRA's Literature for Adolescents Committee and, most recently, the Young Adults' Choices Special Project group members. Many people in many different locations participated. In 1993 team leaders were Anne L. Kenney (Peterborough, New Hampshire), Gail Huffman (Murrysville, Pennsylvania), Jo Ellen Ham (Winnetka, Illinois), Lori Morgan (Anaheim, California), and Jane Owen (Fort Worth, Texas). In 1994 team leaders were Gail Huffman (Murrysville, Pennsylvania), Jo Ellen Ham (Winnetka, Illinois), Virginia Bryg and Dianne Sedlacek (Omaha, Nebraska), Belinda Louie and Cicely Cerqui (Tacoma and Seattle, Washington), and Marilyn Schamroth and Eugenie Stahl (Rockaway, Corona, and Elmhurst, New York). In 1995 team leaders were Grace A. Balwit (Peshtigo, Wisconsin), Christina E. (Beth) Scheiber (Okarche, Oklahoma), Virginia Bryg and Dianne Sedlacek (Omaha, Nebraska), Belinda Louie and Cicely Cerqui (Tacoma and Seattle, Washington), and Marilyn Schamroth and Eugenie Stahl (Hewlett and Forest Hills, New York).

ISBN 0-87207-149-9

Contents

Introduction

Considering the turbulence of adolescence and all the things occupying teenagers' time and attention, it's not surprising that many teens put a low priority on reading—"Who's got time to read?"

More Teens' Favorite Books can help make the job of encouraging adolescents to read for pleasure less of a challenge. This list can be used by anyone who is looking for a book that will grab and hold the interest of a teenager. What makes *More Teens' Favorite Books* unique is that the books included in this three-year compilation were selected by teens themselves as part of the annual project "Young Adults' Choices," sponsored by the International Reading Association. All the books described have been teen-tested by thousands of nature's toughest critics. Whose recommendations are other teens more likely to listen to?

More Teens' Favorite Books includes books appropriate for young adult readers, complete with bibliographic information, annotations, and author and title indexes for easy reference. Teens, like all readers, go through phases—some may read mysteries exclusively for a while, and others may prefer adventure stories or science fiction. With this in mind, entries are grouped by type or genre of publication to make books of a particular interest easy to find. Both fiction and nonfiction books can be found in the categories of history, health, sports, mystery and crime, family life, adventure, and the most popular theme, personal growth. Romance and friendship, science fiction, and fantasy and the supernatural round out the fiction books; the nonfiction books include biographies and nature and ecology.

Many of the books can be used to encourage discussion about how teens can solve personal problems or to foster explorations of current themes and topics. Writing responses can give students an opportunity to explore alternatives in solving problems. Book talks and reading incentive programs can encourage more students to read the books.

If you are asking yourself how to get teenagers interested in reading for pleasure, you may find ideas and answers in the selection of articles that are included in the supplement, which focus on just that question. These articles are written by those seasoned veterans of the struggle to motivate reluctant readers—teachers. Throughout the articles, you will find the following important points emerging again and again:

- **Provide a wide variety of reading material.**
  The wider the variety, the greater the chance that teens will find something of interest to them. Comics, magazines, newspapers, paperback novels, nonfiction books—in the home and in the classroom—are all important sources of reading pleasure and can be the initial step toward young adult literature and a lifetime of reading enjoyment.

- **Respect teens' book selection.**
  Teens' choices of reading material must be respected. Their selections may not always meet the approval of teachers or parents; however, as they gain experience reading for pleasure and confidence in their choices, they may begin to select quality reading materials like the young adult literature listed in *More Teens' Favorite Books*.

- **Provide time for reading.**
  This is important in both the classroom and the home. As little as fifteen minutes a day set aside for pleasure reading can instill and maintain the reading habit in young adults.

- **Read aloud.**
  Try reading aloud part of a *More Teens' Favorite Books* selection. For instance, choose a book with a great beginning to create interest in what happens next, or read aloud a particularly exciting or interesting segment from the middle of a book to capture students' interest in reading the entire book. Then have the books available for them to finish reading on their own.

By keeping this source of ideas and favorite books handy, you will find it easier to encourage pleasure reading in the most reluctant readers.

Adventure

The Fire-Raiser
Maurice Gee. Houghton Mifflin. ISBN 0-395-62428-2.
YAC '94.

> In 1915 an arsonist is loose in a small New Zealand town.
> Four young people from diverse backgrounds pull together to
> stop this terrorist. The backdrop of World War I is personal-
> ized in the prejudice and violence of the townspeople. This is
> a well-crafted novel of adventure and mystery, of psychology
> and friendship.

The Fledglings
Sandra Markle. Bantam. ISBN 0-553-07729-5. YAC '94.

> Orphaned at age 14, Kate runs away to find the grandfather
> she has never known. Surprised to learn he's a Cherokee
> Indian, Kate breaks down his defenses by studying the lan-
> guage and culture and by helping to save an eaglet from
> poachers. Although somewhat simplistic in its treatment, this
> is an exciting adventure story that can be used with units on
> Native American culture and endangered species.

Homebird
Terence Blacker. Bradbury Press. ISBN 0-02-710685-3.
YAC '95.

> This fast-paced story gives a close look at the seamy side of
> life in present-day London. Thirteen-year-old Nicky runs
> away from boarding school, joins some squatters, and be-

comes an apprentice in crime, but finally he returns to his family. Teens whose parents are separated will relate to this story.

The Initiation
Dian Curtis Regan. Avon. ISBN 0-380-76325-7 (paperback). YAC '95.

This adventure story has all the elements of exciting reading for teenagers: danger, ghosts, and romance. Even the most reluctant reader will enjoy this fascinating legend.

I Am Regina
Sally M. Keehn. Philomel. ISBN 0-399-21797-5. YAC '93.

In this fictionalized account of a true story, Regina Leininger is captured and raised by Allegheny Indians in the 1700s. This story can be compared to others books about this complex period of American history. Students could keep a diary of Regina's experiences.

Mercy Hospital: The Best Medicine
Carolyn Carlyle. Avon. ISBN 0-380-76847-X (paperback). YAC '95.

Bernie, Nicole, and Shelley sign up as junior volunteers at Mercy Hospital and get involved in the exciting life-and-death drama of a busy hospital. As they help people they discover that it's not just the doctors who prescribe the best medicine.

Quiver River
David Carkeet. HarperCollins. ISBN 0-06-022454-1. YAC '93.

Carkeet demonstrates a keen ear for teen dialogue and an understanding of the young adult preoccupation with the opposite sex in this funny sequel to The Silent Treatment. This time Ricky Appleton and his friend Nate are working at a camp for the summer. The nearby mountains slowly reveal to Ricky some of the secrets of the Native American tribe that once

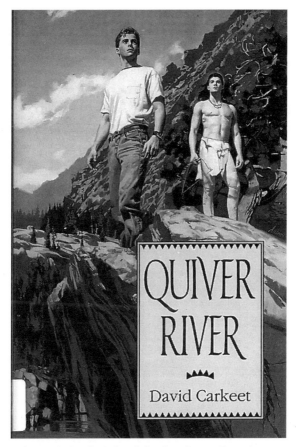

Jacket art ©1991 by Robert Sabin from Quiver River by
David Carkeet.

populated the area. Clever foreshadowing keeps the reader
turning pages enthusiastically.

To the Summit

Claire Rudolf Murphy. Lodestar. ISBN 0-525-67383-0.
YAC '94.

> Seventeen-year-old Sarah Janson faces not only the physical
> challenges of climbing Denali but also the conflicting emo-
> tions surrounding her uneasy relationship with her father,

who is also making the climb. This is a terrific survival/
adventure story with a wonderful heroine who should appeal
to even reluctant readers.

The Wreck of the Barque Stefano Off the North West Cape of Australia in 1875
Gustave Rathe. Farrar, Straus & Giroux. ISBN 0-374-38585-8. YAC '94.

> The author, grandson of one of the two survivors, gives a fic-
> tionalized account of an actual 1875 shipwreck off the north-
> west coast of Australia. Two boys spent almost a year in Aus-
> tralia before they were rescued. This adventurous story gives
> the reader an understanding of Aboriginal culture and can be
> compared to other survival novels.

Biography

Famous Firsts of Black Women
Martha Ward Plowden. Illustrated by Ronald Jones. Pelican.
ISBN 088289-973-2. YAC '95.

> Twenty biographical sketches of African American women
> from the 1700s to the present portray their achievements. As
> the first African American women in their chosen fields, they
> significantly influenced U.S. history. Their dreams and vi-
> sions could inspire young readers today to break through
> cultural and gender barriers.

Lucille Ball: Pioneer of Comedy
Katherine E. Krohn. Lerner. ISBN 0-8225-0603-2. First Avenue Editions. ISBN 0-8225-9603-2 (paperback). YAC '94.

> This biography describes the trials and tribulations of the
> most famous redhead of all. Lucille Ball's tenacity and spirit
> coupled with the simple format of the book could motivate
> students to write their own sketches of other figures from
> popular culture.

Malcolm X: Black Rage
David R. Collins. Dillon. ISBN 0-87518-498-7. YAC '94.

> This biography of the noted black Muslim leader opens with
> the day of his assassination and then looks back on his life in
> the years before he was sentenced to prison. Students should
> be encouraged to read more books about him and compare
> the information.

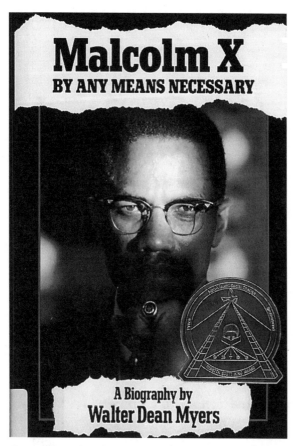

Malcolm X
BY ANY MEANS NECESSARY

A Biography by
Walter Dean Myers

Cover photo © by John Launois/Black Star. Reproduced by
permission of Scholastic Hardcover

Malcolm X: By Any Means Necessary
Walter Dean Myers. Scholastic. ISBN 0-590-46484-1. ISBN
0-590-48109-6 (paperback). YAC '95.

This biography of the civil rights activist portrays a complex
man who rises from thief to religious leader, preaching against
racism and for human rights. The book portrays the 1960s as
a tumultuous time of assassinations as well as legacies of freedom and hope.

Rosa Parks: My Story

Rosa Parks with Jim Haskins. Dial. ISBN 0-8037-0673-1. YAC '94.

> Biography of the woman whose refusal to give up her seat on a Montgomery, Alabama, bus on December 1, 1955, sparked a nationwide civil rights movement.

Family Life

Crosstown
Kathryn Makris. Avon. ISBN 0-380-76226-9 (paperback). YAC '95.

> Fifteen-year-old April's world falls apart when she finds out that she and her brother and mother have to move from the shelter of suburbia to the urban unknown. Any teenager who has had to move or has gone through a bitter divorce in the family should be able to relate to this coming-of-age novel.

Family of Strangers
Susan Beth Pfeffer. Bantam. ISBN 0-533-08364-3. Laurel Leaf/Bantam Doubleday Dell. ISBN 0-440-21895-0 (paperback). YAC '94.

> In this realistic story, a 16-year-old girl writes imaginary dialogues and letters as a way of coping with her dysfunctional family. After she attempts suicide, a therapist helps her find courage and hope for the future. The book's writing samples can serve as models for student writing.

The Rain Catchers
Jean Thesman. Houghton Mifflin. ISBN 0-395-55333-4. Avon. ISBN 0-380-71711-5 (paperback). YAC '93.

> Fourteen-year-old Grayling has grown up in her grandmother's home in Seattle surrounded by professional women who create stories, minister to the sick, and succeed in business. But Grayling wonders why her mother, a successful businesswoman in San Francisco, has never wanted Grayling to live

with her. Grayling's feelings about best friends, first romance, the dangers of living in a large city, and the death of an adult friend are revealed. The importance of intergenerational experiences for children and adolescents is explored.

Shiloh
Phyllis Reynolds Naylor. Atheneum. ISBN 0-689-31614-3. YAC '93.

A stray hunting dog, an abused beagle belonging to the callous and mean Judd Travers, sets off a series of events that challenge 11-year-old Marty Preston's courage and sense of decency. He meets those challenges and earns the respect of his family and, grudgingly, of Judd. *Skeeter, The Far Side of the Mountain*, and *The Biscuit Eater* could also be read to help students understand humans' love for animals and the role animals play in fostering maturity.

Summer Girl
Deborah Moulton. Dial. ISBN 0-8037-1153-0. YAC '94.

When her mother is dying, Tommy is sent to live with her father, from whom she has not heard since her parents' divorce. Ten years of separation have built up resentment and misunderstanding in Tommy's heart. Students might discuss and compare this with other titles on divorce, illness, and death.

Teenage Fathers
Karen Gravelle and Leslie Peterson. Messner. ISBN 0-671-72850-4. ISBN 0-671-72851-2 (paperback). YAC '94.

Thirteen case studies explore teenage boys' feelings about being fathers. Their situations vary greatly—from irresponsible Carlos, father of nine children by the age of 19, to Wayne, who continues to work hard at his relationship with his 3-year-old daughter and her mother. One young reader responded: "After reading about the difficulties faced by teenage fathers, I see it is not a good idea to have children at a young age."

What Daddy Did

Neal Shusterman. Little, Brown. ISBN 0-316-78906-2. Harper Keypoint. ISBN 0-06-447094-6. YAC '93.

> Preston Scott knew that his parents were having marital problems, but he didn't think that his father would kill his mother! This powerful novel recounts Preston's psychological journey from the despair of losing his mother to the painful rebuilding of his shattered relationship with his father.

Wolf at the Door

Barbara Corcoran. Atheneum/Simon & Schuster Children's Publishing. ISBN 0-689-31870-7. YAC '95.

> Lee feels overshadowed by her younger sister, an aspiring actress. When she begins observing a wolf pack on her family's Montana wilderness property, she finds her own artistic strengths: drawing pictures of the wolves and writing about their behavior. This novel can be used with units on coming-of-age or family relationships, as well as studies on endangered animals.

Supplement:
Reading for Pleasure

- ### The Reader's Bill of Rights
  Daniel Pennac, translated by David Homel
  From *Better Than Life*, Daniel Pennac. Trans. David Homel, 1994. :
  Toronto: Coach House Press.

- ### A "Fiver" for a Book
  Bobbi Swiderek
  Adapted from *Journal of Adolescent & Adult Literacy*, *39*(1),
  September 1995.

- ### Free-Choice Reading?
  ### Are You Kidding?
  Mary Jo Sherman
  Adapted from *SIGNAL Journal*, *19*(3), Spring/Summer 1995.

- ### Encouraging the
  ### Lifetime Reading Habit
  Joseph Sanacore
  Adapted from *Journal of Reading*, *35*(6), March 1992.

The Reader's Bill of Rights

1. THE RIGHT TO NOT READ

2. THE RIGHT TO SKIP PAGES

3. THE RIGHT TO NOT FINISH

4. THE RIGHT TO REREAD

5. THE RIGHT TO READ ANYTHING

6. THE RIGHT TO ESCAPISM

7. THE RIGHT TO READ ANYWHERE

8. THE RIGHT TO BROWSE

9. THE RIGHT TO READ OUT LOUD

10. THE RIGHT TO NOT DEFEND YOUR TASTES

These are the rights that we grant ourselves;
these are the rights we must grant young readers.

[From Better Than Life, Daniel Pennac. Trans. David Homel, 1994. Toronto: Coach House Press. Reviewed by Judith E. Zolman, Journal of Reading, 38(8), May 1995.]

A "Fiver" for a Book

Bobbi Swiderek

The author has taught for 18 years at the elementary and middle school levels. She is the "Middle School" columnist for the first volume year of the Journal of Adolescent & Adult Literacy *and is currently working toward a graduate degree in middle school education.*

About a year ago I happened upon an interview with the actor Nick Nolte in which he commented that he did not discover books until he left school. Athletics—not academics—had kept him in school, but he wondered why his alma maters had not given students the time to read and the choice of material. I keep Nick Nolte in mind when I justify my reading program. I let kids read self-selected material every day for most of the class period and assign no book reports. (We do keep reading logs.) Nick Nolte might find today's middle school more appealing.

Reading has always been my favorite pastime, but that's not so unusual for my generation. Television arrived when I was seven—clear reception (mainly in the form of a test pattern) came two years later. We had plenty of time for reading then—not so now. Today, adolescent literature is better than ever. If we are to compete with Nintendo, MTV, and the Internet, teachers must allow students to read books—in school—on a daily basis. Not only must we allow them to read, but we sometimes must entice them to read.

Anyone who has taught nearly two decades (as I have) realizes that every teaching format has a wrinkle or two to iron out. My wrinkles are reluctant readers. Do you have such students in your classrooms? They are quite easy to identify. Mostly boys, but sometimes girls, these students are always choosing or returning (not reading) books during the sustained silent reading period. When forbidden to frequent the library, reluctant readers will leave their books at home...or in their lockers...or in another classroom...or anywhere!

The reluctant readers are quite intelligent. Not only are they clever at misplacing books for class, but they have sometimes used this tactic to their financial advantage. Occasionally, one of these clever souls will borrow a book that I have borrowed from the district library in hopes of enticing them to read. When the book is long overdue (and in my name), I will frantically start a quest for the book. Since I am somewhat abstract random (that's one of Tony Gregorc's four learning styles; the other three are concrete random, abstract sequential, and concrete sequential), I often do not write down the borrower's name; hence I don't know which student to accost. Everyone assures me they've looked everywhere and can't find the book. Finally, in desperation (and to save my hide from the district librarian who has never lost a book), I offer a reward of $5 for the return of the book. Within hours (many times, within minutes), the book is on my desk and the reluctant reader is pocketing the "fiver" while asking for a pass to the library—to get a book for class, of course!

How does one motivate these elusive readers? (Hmmm, I believe there was a paragraph or two on this in my undergraduate methods classes.) I've had to rely on my kid-watching skills and some trial and error refinement to develop some strategies to lure these folks to the "reading trough." Someone once wrote that the key to management was Location, Location, Location. I think the key to motivation is twofold: Timing, Timing, Timing, and Conning, Conning, Conning.

- Con 1: The Read

    Read to your class. This is simple, but it works. If a book is particularly slow in parts, paraphrase, condense, or move to the exciting sections. Leave kids dangling each day if possible. Don't be afraid to read books that need on-the-spot editing or omissions.

    Caution: Alert substitute teachers if a book needs on-the-spot editing. (Once I forgot to do this; the poor woman plowed right through four-letter expletives before she realized what she was doing!)

- Con 2: The Swear

Middle schoolers are fascinated with swear words and they delight in reading such language in script other than their own. One time I was trying to interest a boy in a book that I knew he would like. He kept shaking his head, no. I said "You're probably right. Besides the book has swearing in it." I put the book back on the shelf and walked away. Two weeks later he appeared at my desk with the book.

"Ms. Swiderek, I read this book twice and I couldn't find any swear words." I reached for the book, slowly perused a page or two, then said "Oh, I had that book mixed up with this one." I handed him a copy of *The Last Mission* by Harry Mazer.

Caution: Make sure the second book has a swear word or two. Some mistakes, kids make only once.

- Con 3: The Tease

The Tease is easy to do and, unlike the Swear, you can repeat it over and over. One form is the book talk. Another method is to read a book silently (while the kids read), then say each day, "Listen to this. I can't believe this." Then read a paragraph or two. I did this with *They Cage the Animals at Night* by Jennings M. Burch, and kids began pestering me to finish the book so they could read it.

Caution: This method could cost you money. I purchased an additional copy of this book for a student who tried to borrow it from several libraries. He was hooked, and I was afraid his interest would wane before the library copy became available.

- Con 4: The Forbidden

The quickest way to pique 12- to 14-year-olds' interest is to forbid them to do something. Each year I omit one chapter in Torey Hayden's *One Child* when I read it aloud. I stop, look up, say very seriously, "I won't be able to read this chapter because your parents might object." One boy announced in another class that he was going to read the section when I left for lunch. I locked the book in my file cabinet so he couldn't get it. I also kept my book mark 20 pages before my place so that a student couldn't locate the forbidden passage too easily.

I used the Forbidden with Robert Cormier's books. I read *We All Fall Down* and then removed it from my bookshelves. I told the students it was "too violent." Several students read every Robert Cormier book in the library trying to locate the book. (One student—a year later and in eighth grade—finally did locate it and came in to tell me he'd read that book!)

Sometimes I pull a book out, glance at it, then say, "No, you can't read this until you're in eighth grade." (One student had his mom write me a note insisting that he be allowed to read the book in seventh grade.) When all else fails, turn to R.L. Stine or Gary Paulsen. They're masters at enticing the most reluctant middle school readers.

Titles Mentioned
Burch, Jennings M. (1985.). *They cage the animals at night.* New York: NAL-Dutton.
Cormier, Robert. (1991.). *We all fall down.* New York: Delacorte.
Hayden, Torey. (1981.). *One child.* New York: Avon.
Mazer, Harry. (1981.). *The last mission.* New York: Dell.

Free-Choice Reading? Are You Kidding?

Mary Jo Sherman

*The author has taught seventh grade
reading/language arts for 33 years. She is chair of
IRA's Special Interest Group on Adolescent Literature:
SIGNAL, was president of IRA's Middle School
Reading Special Interest Group for three years, and is
a past winner of IRA's Nila Banton Smith Award for
Content Area Reading.*

From the time I graduated from college in 1963 with an English major, I was positive I knew what my students should read. After all, if I didn't, who did? I'm sure that many of my students saw that raised eyebrow, that look down my nose, as I glanced at what they'd chosen. In an individualized reading program, I set very clear guidelines for the books I'd approve: 150 pages or longer, approximately at the student's reading level, and without the "F word" and its relatives. I scrupulously maintained my list of the "blessed"—and heaven help the students whose book wasn't recorded on my trusty list. Students and parents would occasionally call me at home to make sure a particular book was satisfactory. What power!

Then in my 29th year of teaching, I read *In the Middle* by Nancie Atwell, followed closely by Linda Rief's *Seeking Diversity*. They presented a very different viewpoint. The whole workshop approach made sense. I wanted to try it, but I knew I needed to "buy" the whole package to give it a fair trial and that meant letting my students select what they read. Was I ready to give up prescribing what I was sure was right for a given student? How could they survive? Finally, I decided I could experiment for nine weeks, give the new idea a chance to flop, see what happened, pick up after the damage and failure, and return to "my list" for the rest of the year—no (or very little) harm done.

A year and a half and more than 300 students later, the only harm done has been to my self-assurance. It was miraculous—I've seen too many cases for it to be a fluke. Self-selection really does work, and the best thing, the real pay-off, is that students become readers. It still amazes me to read in a student's reading journal how she thinks R.L. Stine is too predictable now and that Lois Duncan is more her style. More than one young woman has found her way to Cynthia Voigt and Torey Hayden, not because I forced the journey, but because she tired of the less challenging authors. Seventh grade boys who don't consider them-selves readers at the beginning find their way from Stine's *Goosebumps*; to Spinelli's *Maniac Magee* (which still brings tears to my eyes after many readings); to *Space Station Seventh Grade*, through the superb prose of Gary Paulsen; and finally to Remarque's *All Quiet on the West-ern Front*, Magorian's *Good Night, Mr. Tom*, and Piers Paul Read's *Alive!* and similar titles, as they come back to me later to recommend other authors they've discovered.

In the beginning I had no idea what it took, but I'm figuring it out. Nerve and self-control. All kidding aside, first, students have to have ac-cess to books. A school library will work, but I never realized what im-pact a classroom library would have on students. Does it make the media center people happy? No, but it makes magic for my students. My collec-tion numbers about 450 titles now, thanks to a generous principal and my sharing my own allowance. Who needs more earrings anyway? My principal says he gets more return on his dollars in my classroom collec-tion than anywhere else he spends money, and the presence of the books in the classroom creates a fantastic atmosphere. Do the students have to get their books from my classroom collection? Absolutely not, and I try very hard to treat all books equally. Oh, if the book's really smarmy, I'll ask the student to bring me a note from parents, saying they're aware that Junior is reading it, but they can read anything they choose. I try to make sure my collection covers a wide range, but I surely don't have everything. I don't want everything! One of my favorite experiences was seeing a boy last year carrying around *The Stand* by Stephen King, out where everyone could see—a big hardback edition that really made a statement—but inside his notebook was always a paperback copy of some heart-warming dog story that he was actually reading.

Second, the teacher needs to be an avid reader of young adult (YA) books. Seeing a teacher reading "their" books is far more powerful for students than being told reading's important. It's not something that can be faked by reading a plot summary. If the students believe the teacher reads avidly, they'll share their opinions about the titles the teacher hasn't read yet. I can't count the times that a student has taken me by the arm, led me to the bookcases, and given me a book talk on his or her favorite title, closing with putting the book in my hand and looking straight in my eyes—I get the message! Read it! Just last week a girl I never would have "pegged" as a reader assigned me Martha Humphrey's *Until Whatever*. I can't wait to talk to her on Monday—what a book! And she's probably hooked on reading forever. What fun I've had reading Paulsen's *Hatchet* (and his *Nightjohn* should be required reading for the human race—the final chapter is so lyrical I sat in my empty classroom and read it aloud), anything by Spinelli, Walter Dean Myers' *Fallen Angels* (only after I heard Myers explain why he wrote it—I still get shivers when I think of it), Barron's *Heartlight*, Voigt's *Wings of a Falcon*, Hamilton's *House of Dies Drear* and its sequel *The Mystery of Drear House*. They're my "books of choice" now, with only occasional detours to adult fiction to be inspired by Annie Dillard, Wallace Stegner, and Jane Smiley. Dillard herself wrote that writers have to be careful what they read because it has an impact on how they write—and I'd add—on what they become. Young adult fiction keeps me in touch with real human values, with fantastic writing, and with my students. I could go on and on about what YA reading has done for me—can you tell?

Third, as long as we assign grades, there has to be a method of evaluation, which means there has to be an exchange of information—an individual, private conversation about books, where there's no pressure like there is on book reports, but where there's an honest sharing of opinions and a forthright connection of books with life. In my classroom, the reading journals fill this need.

The "germ" of this idea came from *In the Middle* by Nancie Atwell when she wrote about creating her dining room table in her classroom, so that she and her students could have literate conversations about reading, gossiping about the authors, comparing various works, etc., in the notes in their reading logs. Linda Rief added refinements in *Seeking Diversity*. It all sounded too simple, too sensible to work, and I had lots of concern about accountability. Who was writing what to whom? How could I cope with more writing? I needn't have worried.

Simply put, my students and I have rediscovered letter writing. Each week my students have two days of reading workshop where they read. They may spend their time one of those days writing their reading log letter for the week, but most do that at home (once they get into it, they say they want to be able to concentrate on the letters at home). Each student is required to write a letter a week and have it answered. All letters must be in ink, bound in the log consecutively, and about their reading. Since I teach three language arts classes, I have the letters on a three-week rotation. One week the student writes a letter to a friend (initially a classmate); the friend writes back on the next log page. The next week the student writes to a family member and that person writes back. The third week, the student writes to me and I write back, so each week I get logs from one class. Although I write more than 25 letters a week, it is the most satisfying thing I do with my students, and it emphasizes to them that I'm a reader and a writer, too.

- Requirements: (1) students who are given time to read; (2) a teacher who is a reader (especially of YA literature) and will write letters; and (3) parents who are willing to write letters every three weeks.
- Materials: (1) one hefty spiral notebook that can last the year; (2) various teacher-generated and adapted forms; and (3) access to books.

In the beginning they do it because they have to; but with the combination of class time to read, the fact that they choose what they read, and the free-wheeling format of the letters, they are soon writing page-long letters in which they reflect on what they read. In my letters back to them, I try to draw further connections mentioning books I know may follow the same theme, or I share with them books that have been and are particularly meaningful to me. As the year progresses, the letters evolve into literate conversations. Friends see each other in a new light through the letters; they write to me that they've made new friends through the letters. They give each other recommendations, and the books make the rounds from one friend to another. Many parents (and students, too) have told me that the logs have become part of their family archives, saving for all time the reflections of the maturing young adult. Many times the family letter back to the student closes with this line: "I am so proud of you. I am so happy you're enjoying reading—and I love you very much."

Is it a perfect world? Are you kidding? There are still weak moments when I want to assign a particular student to a particular book, but now I know that if it's meant to be, the two of them will get together on their own—and the bond will be permanent. I try very hard to shut my mouth unless I'm asked for a recommendation, and even then I go slowly. Last year a really bright seventh grade girl went from one silly romance book to another, having little to reflect on in her reading journal because there was little to reflect on from the books. How badly I wanted to say, "Why don't you try...?" I just knew she needed my input, but I bit my lip for a month, and finally she asked for the first recommendation. What a reader she has become, and her writing has improved immensely as a result. But if I had butted in with some unsought recommendation, she'd probably still be clinging to her old familiar choices out of spite.

I'm not one to cast off my old way of doing things easily or willingly, but I'm all too happy to declare that I have probably helped more students become readers in the past year and a half than in my entire previous teaching career—and these readers write—and most often write correctly, and that's the whole purpose of teaching language arts, isn't it?

Titles Mentioned

Atwell, Nancie. (1987). *In the middle: Writing, reading, and learning with adolescents.* Portsmouth, NH: Heinemann/Boynton/Cook.
Barron, T.A. (1990). *Heartlight.* Philomel.
Hamilton, Virginia. (1968). *House of Dies Drear.* New York: Macmillan.
Hamilton, Virginia. (1987). *The mystery of Drear House: The conclusion of the Dies Drear chronicle.* New York: Greenwillow.
Humphrey, Martha. (1991). *Until whatever.* New York: Clarion.
King, Stephen. (1978). *The stand.* New York: Doubleday.
Leonhardt, Mary. (1992). *Parents who love reading, kids who don't.* New York: Crown Publishing.
Magorian, Michelle. (1981). *Good night, Mr. Tom.* New York: Harper.
Myers, Walter Dean. (1988). *Fallen angels.* New York: Scholastic.
Paulsen, Gary. (1987). *Hatchet.* New York: Bradbury.
Paulsen, Gary. (1993). *Nightjohn.* New York: Delacorte.
Read, Piers Paul. (1979). *Alive!: The story of the Andes survivors.* New York: Avon.

Remarque, Erich M. (1929). *All quiet on the western front*. New York: Little, Brown.

Rief, Linda. (1992). *Seeking diversity*. Portsmouth, NH: Heinemann/Boynton, Cook.

Spinelli, Jerry. (1990). *Maniac Magee*. Boston: Little, Brown.

Spinelli, Jerry. (1982). *Space station seventh grade*. Boston: Little, Brown.

Voigt, Cynthia. (1993). *Wings of a falcon*. New York: Scholastic.

Encouraging the Lifetime Reading Habit

Joseph Sanacore

The author taught elementary and secondary school for 12 years and was a K–12 language arts administrator for 21 years. He is presently a columnist for the Journal of Adolescent & Adult Literacy *and executive director of the National Center for Improving the Culture of Schools.*

What can we do to promote lifetime literacy? Can we justify using school time for developing the habit of reading? If so, how do we balance the rest of the language arts curriculum and also fulfill external requirements?

A dilemma seems to exist in schools. While we know the importance of supporting lifetime literacy, we tend to become frustrated about not having enough time in school to attain this goal. We not only feel the pressure of fulfilling much of the language arts curriculum, but also encounter the stress of meeting state education department mandates such as testing. Because an extensive testing frenzy exists throughout the United States, it is not surprising that we feel sandwiched between what we know we must do to promote lifetime literacy and what we consider to be less important demands that fragment teaching and learning.

Compounding this dilemma is an important question concerning teacher empowerment: Who is driving language arts instruction? If we continue to succumb to external mandates, we are likely to emphasize teacher-directed activities that support testing outcomes. We also might be coerced into believing that using school time for encouraging a love of reading is a waste of time. This diminishing control of our decision making could translate into our students' loss of ownership concerning their lifetime literacy. Described another way, if we are not permitted to encourage independent reading in school because it is considered a frill, then our students will not experience a sense of ownership in selecting books that they want to read. They also will be denied the opportunity to develop the lifetime reading habit.

Independent reading, which is one way of supporting lifetime literacy, is not a frill. It can help students to refine skills and strategies by applying them to meaningful text (expository, descriptive, narrative). It also can help readers build their prior knowledge of different topics and improve their reading achievement through the natural process of reading. As important, independent reading motivates a love of reading as it supports the habit of reading (Sanacore, 1988, 1989a).

During the past decade, I have become increasingly aware of the need to use school time for encouraging the reading habit. I have observed demographic trends that indicate many of our students are living in homes with two working parents or with a single parent who must work. Thus, a number of our students enter homes each afternoon with little or no adult supervision. At the least, they probably become involved in too much television viewing, too much telephone conversation, and other activities that displace reading for pleasure. Over time, they are more at risk of failing, of becoming illiterate or aliterate, and of dropping out of school.

Since our students are not likely to do much pleasure reading at home, we must accept the challenge of encouraging the lifetime reading habit in school. Although independent reading is not a panacea, it represents an important step toward enhancing literacy for students and for society (Sanacore, 1989b). Let us consider the following ways of creating lifelong readers.

Clutter up the classroom. If we surround students with books, newspapers, magazines, and other materials, they will be tempted to browse and to read some of these sources. When selecting materials for the classroom, we should work closely with the library media specialist because he or she is usually aware of a wide variety of materials that are well matched with students' interests and needs.

Cooperatively, we can clutter up the classroom so that our students have the opportunity to select their own material and to develop the habit of reading for pleasure. Over time, as we respect their choices and encourage their reading, our students will realize that particular books have a unique impact on them. For example, there are books that create emotional and sensory responses, that stimulate the imagination, that trigger new interests, that give solace, and that spark new directions.

In reviewing reading autobiographies of lifelong readers, Carlsen and Sherrill (1988) found that rarely was a book's appeal associated with its degree of literary merit. Often, what the autobiographer "remembered was the emotional impact of the book, the insights it provided whether for self or others, and the growth that it stimulated in the reading. The writers of the autobiographies described books as kindling the imagination, creating visions of life's possibilities, giving expression to the readers' own inarticulate feelings, as well as affecting their emotions, intellectual pursuits, and attitudes. In this way, books provide readers with a continuing, evolving view of both themselves and the world" (p. 86).

These findings help us to understand the importance of providing students with a wide variety of reading materials. They also remind us to respect our students' choices because reasons other than literary merit seem to be associated with a desire to read.

Although we sometimes become anxious about our students' choices, Nell (1988) reminds us that as readers gain experience reading for pleasure, they tend to select appropriate materials. This positive experience with reading builds independence and self-esteem, both of which are important for creating lifelong readers (Sanacore, 1990).

Provide time for reading. A classroom cluttered with reading materials sets the stage for effective independent reading. What we must do now is give our students the opportunity to read for pleasure in the classroom. Those of us who are risk-takers will organize instructional activities during the school year so that a major block of time is devoted to independent reading. In this plan, our students are immersed in the reading of interesting materials each day for about five weeks. They come to class, select books on their own, and read at their own comfortable pace.

Our roles include securing a wide diversity of materials for our students and, upon request, providing guidance with book selection and with comprehension.

While our students are reading, we should also be reading. We should not be correcting papers, planning lessons, or doing other clerical tasks. Our students will consider their reading immersion to be more important if they see us demonstrating the joy of reading too.

Because of current demographic trends, societal pressures, and testing mandates (Sanacore, 1989c), our students are more at risk of failing to become lifelong learners. By providing them with time to read in school, we are sending them a message that lifetime literacy is a major instructional activity.

As language arts teachers, we should be concerned not only with promoting lifetime literacy in our classrooms but also with supporting its value across the curriculum. We should be taking an active role in cooperating with our content area colleagues to stimulate independent reading in their classrooms. Without such schoolwide efforts, our students are likely to believe that reading for pleasure is an acceptable activity only in language arts classes. On the contrary, they should experience the excitement of reading a diversity of materials in a variety of content area classes.

One way of supporting this challenging goal is to guide content area colleagues to include independent reading in their classrooms for sustained blocks of time. For example, an English teacher might help a social studies colleague incorporate independent reading into a unit focusing on World War II. At first, the English teacher might suggest that the textbook be used for covering important aspects of the war. When the social studies teacher is confident that essential information has been covered, the English teacher can make suggestions about other materials that poignantly deal with World War II. Thus, Corrie ten Boom's *The Hiding Place*, Bette Greene's *Summer of My German Soldier*, and *Anne Frank: The Diary of a Young Girl* might be among the recommended literature that students can appreciate reading in social studies classrooms. During the selection of such literature, the library media specialist can serve as a vital resource.

By initially encouraging a content area colleague to use his or her textbook, the English teacher is demonstrating respect for a dominant resource used in that subject area. By then suggesting works of literature, the English teacher is sensitively easing the colleague into experimenting with other materials for helping students learn about an instructional unit.

The more challenging task, however, is motivating the colleague to use a major block of time for reading about World War II. We probably can provide such motivation in the form of supportive information, For example, 5 weeks of independent reading provide the teacher and students with 35 weeks for other instructional activities and quizzes. Thus, independent reading does not significantly impose on other important curricular areas (Sanacore, 1988). This is particularly true if teachers agree to alternate the times they provide for independent reading, so that students experience it in different classes at different times of the year.

We also should discuss with the colleague research findings, such as that reading for pleasure is significantly linked to the amount of leisure time engaged in reading (Greaney & Hegarty, 1987), and this in turn is linked to reading achievement (Greaney, 1980). This information, by itself, is no guarantee that the colleague will include independent reading in the social studies classroom; however, a reasonable professional will at least consider adapting or experimenting with a new idea if he or she is made aware of supportive information (Morrow, 1986; Sanacore, 1989a).

Throughout this experimental period, we all must constantly remind ourselves that the purpose of this bold approach is to help our students realize that our content areas are informational as well as interesting. Our ultimate goal, of course, is to have virtually every content area teacher supporting the lifetime reading habit.

With no naiveté intended, our efforts to promote a love of reading may result in former students visiting us and saying "Thanks to your support, I continue to read for pleasure!"

Encourage the reading habit throughout the school year. In addition to extended blocks of time for independent reading, we should promote opportunities for reading as often as possible. Thus, the habit of reading will become part of our students' lifestyle.

According to Trelease (1989a, 1989b), when we regularly read aloud to our students, they have continuous exposure to a wide variety of books, richly textured experiences, extensive vocabulary, new information, a good reading role model, and the pleasures of reading. Matthews (1987) believes that the read-aloud atmosphere should be warm, intimate, and trusting and that the teacher should select powerful passages that stimulate responses to the ideas presented. If copies of the resources we read aloud are available in the classroom clutter and if we provide class time for reading, our students are more apt to read these resources.

About 15 minutes of silent reading several days a week are probably sufficient. As our students become absorbed in their selections, they might continue reading them at home.

Another way of promoting the love of reading is through a booktalk. A talk that is well presented is entertaining as well as enticing. Its main purpose is to motivate individuals to want to know more about a book (Bodart, 1980). Although school librarians give booktalks as one of their many roles, we can also share our enjoyment of books through frequent talks.

The following suggestions, adapted from Chelton (1976) and Donelson and Nilsen (1989), increase the potential for successful book-talks: (1) Be well prepared so that eye contact is easily maintained. (2) Organize books so that they can be shown during the talk. To lessen confusion, attach a card with pertinent notes on it to the back of each book. (3) Present excerpts that reflect the style and tone of the books. (4) Present a wide variety of books during the school year rather than focus on a limited number of themes. (5) Use different formats, such as some poetry or a short movie. (6) Keep records of the books that have been presented so that before and after circulation figures on the books can be compared.

Although booktalks can motivate a love of reading, the pairing of young adult books with traditional literature can also stimulate a desire to read. According to La Blanc (1980), "These book teams have several advantages over teaching significant literature in isolation. The reader is hooked on the theme by reading the easily manageable adolescent novel first. The more difficult book has the advantage of being based on a familiar theme and is associated with the positive, successful experience of reading the young adult novel" (pp. 35-36).

La Blanc believes that as teenage readers make the connection between young adult literature and its adult counterpart, they are more likely to grow into lifelong readers. Suggested pairings of books include: Irene Hunt's *Across Five Aprils* with Ernest Hemingway's *For Whom the Bell Tolls*, Mildred Taylor's *Roll of Thunder, Hear My Cry* with Harper Lee's *To Kill a Mockingbird* and Sue Ellen Bridger's *Home Before Dark* with John Steinbeck's *The Grapes of Wrath*.

In addition to the pairing of books, we could extend this method to the pairing of authors who are similar in their writing styles or themes. Donelson and Nilsen (1989) suggest that we begin instructional units with an important young adult author, progress to a modern adult writer, and move on to an established author.

For example, students could be exposed to Robert Cormier as a significant writer for young adults, to James Baldwin as an important modern author for adults, and finally to Henrik Ibsen as a major established writer. These three have similarities in their thematic focus (the individual vs. the system) and in their literary focus (development of plot).

The pairing of books and authors can stimulate a desire to read. This method also has the potential for promoting lifetime readers who appreciate a variety of themes and literary styles.

As classroom teachers, we often feel pressured about balancing instructional activities for our students. We attempt to be sensitive to demographic trends, to meet external mandates, and to provide valuable literacy learning experiences. We also know that schools are becoming the major source of lifelong learning. Although our schools cannot be everything to everyone, we must stay committed to supporting lifetime literacy efforts.

Cluttering up the classroom with a wide variety of interesting materials, providing major blocks of time for independent reading, and encouraging the reading habit during the entire school year are three school-wide approaches for promoting lifetime readers. Success with these and other approaches requires the cooperative support of classroom teachers, library media specialists, administrators, and parents. Such support, of course, involves time and hard work, but these efforts will be worth it.

References

Bodart, J. (1980). *Booktalk! Booktalking and school visiting for young adult audiences*. New York: H.W. Wilson.

Carlsen, G., & Sherrill, A. (1988). *Voices of readers: How we come to love books*. Urbana, IL: National Council of Teachers of English.

Chelton, M. (1976). Booktalking: You can do it. *School Library Journal, 22*, 39–43.

Donelson, K., & Nilsen, A.P. (1989). *Literature for today's young adults*. Glenview, IL: Scott, Foresman.

Greaney, V. (1980). Factors related to amount and type of leisure-time reading. *Reading Research Quarterly, 15*, 337–357.

Greaney, V., & Hegarty, M. (1987). Correlates of leisure-time reading. *Journal of Research in Reading, 10*, 3–32.

La Blanc, R. (1980). An English teacher's fantasy. *English Journal, 69*, 35–36.

Matthews, C. (1987). Lap reading for teenagers. *Journal of Reading, 30*, 410–413.

Morrow, L. (1986). Attitudes of teachers, principals, and parents toward promoting voluntary reading in the elementary school. *Reading Research and Instruction, 25*, 116–130.

Nell, V. (1988). *Lost in a book: The psychology of reading for pleasure*. New Haven, CT: Yale University Press.

Sanacore, J. (1988). Schoolwide independent reading: The principal can help. *Journal of Reading, 31*, 346–353.

Sanacore, J. (1989a). Needed: The principal's support in creating a positive professional attitude toward independent reading in the schools. *Reading Research and Instruction, 28*, 73–79.

Sanacore, J. (1989b). Societal pressures and the need for developing lifetime literacy through independent reading in the schools. *The High School Journal, 72*, 130–135.

Sanacore, J. (1990). Creating the lifetime reading habit in social studies. *Journal of Reading, 33*, 414–418.

Trelease, J. (1989a). Jim Trelease speaks on reading aloud to children. *The Reading Teacher, 43*, 200–206.

Trelease, J. (1989b). *The new read-aloud handbook*. New York: Penguin.

Fantasy and the Supernatural

Albion's Dream

Roger Norman. Delacorte. ISBN 0-385-30533-8. YAC '94.

A mysterious board game hidden away for years draws Edward and his cousin into a chilling adventure foreshadowing events in the story. Warned by his father not to play, Edward is powerless to resist the temptation when he realizes the playing cards bear a sinister resemblance to tyrannical figures at his school.

Andra

Louise Lawrence. HarperCollins. ISBN 0-06-023705-8. YAC '93.

Earth is a very different place in 2,000 years: People live underground in environmentally protected cities, society is rigidly controlled, and accidents never occur. When Andra receives a brain graft from a boy who died in 1987, his memories of Earth become hers and she can no longer tolerate her repressed existence. When she incites the young people of

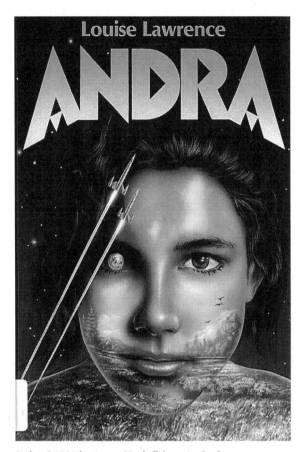

Louise Lawrence

ANDRA

Jacket ©1991 by Anton Kimball from Andra by
Louise Lawrence.

her city to openly rebel, Andra forces change but is betrayed
by a friend. Even teens who don't like science fiction loved
this book.

Dreadful Sorry

Kathryn Reiss. Harcourt Brace (Jovanovich). ISBN 0-15-
224213-9. YAC '95.

In this suspenseful novel, 17-year-old Molly slips into the life
of a young woman who disappeared over 80 years ago. Teens
will be intrigued by the taut plot and supernatural theme.

Dream Spinner
Joanne Hoppe. Morrow. ISBN 0-688-08559-8. YAC '94.

Through dreams, a 15-year-old girl travels back to the 1890s. The reader must decide if they are real journeys or just realistic dreams. Reading this fantasy novel could lead to discussions of real versus make-believe.

Flight of the Dragon Kyn
Susan Fletcher. Atheneum. ISBN 0-689-31880-4. YAC '95.

This action-packed fantasy, a prequel to *Dragon's Milk* (1991), finds 15-year-old Kara caught up in a fierce rivalry between Orrik and his jealous brother Rog. After the death of the dragon that once saved her life, Kara uses her special powers to lead the other dragons to safety.

Hero's Song
Edith Pattou. Harcourt Brace (Jovanovich). ISBN 0-15-233807-1. YAC '93.

This action-packed fantasy portrays a reluctant hero's quest to rescue his kidnapped sister and his struggle to save the kingdom from the Queen of Ghosts, who sends all sorts of magic beasts to stop him. The book can be compared to other books in which good finally triumphs over evil.

Juniper
Monica Furlong. Knopf. ISBN 394-93220. Knopf. ISBN 679-83369 (paperback). YAC '93.

Fantasy woven with realistic emotions makes this medieval story interesting and fast reading. Juniper's gifts for magic are recognized early, but she must learn how to stop her Aunt Meroot from destroying her family and the kingdom. Teachers may use Juniper to introduce or extend units on fantasy, family relationships, or self-knowledge. Students might extend the plot by adding to Juniper's powers or providing additional situations for their use. This is a good story for parents to read or discuss with their children.

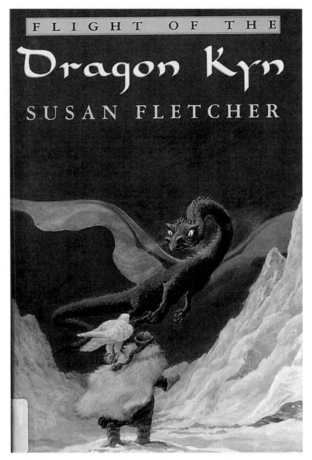

FLIGHT OF THE

Dragon Kyn

SUSAN FLETCHER

Jacket illustration copyright ©1993 by Jos A Smith. Reprinted with the permission of Atheneum Books for Young Readers, an imprint of Simon & Schuster from Flight of the Dragon Kyn by Susan Fletcher. Copyright ©1993 Susan Fletcher.

The Juniper Game
Sherryl Jordan. Scholastic. ISBN-0-590-44728-9. Scholastic. ISBN 0-590-44729-7 (paperback). YAC '93.

> Juniper, age 15, has telepathic powers. She convinces Dylan Pidgley, a quiet, artistic boy, to participate in her experiments. He is able to draw accurate images that Juniper sends him telepathically and is too fascinated to withdraw from the

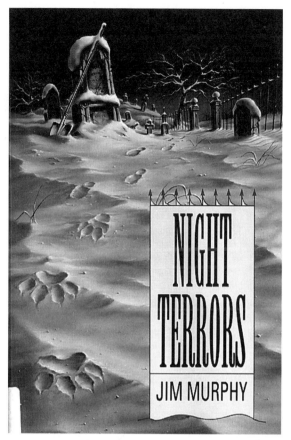

situation. Fantasy lovers will enjoy reading about Juniper's game of life and death.

Night Terrors

Jim Murphy. Scholastic. ISBN 0-590-45341-6. ISBN 0-590-45342-4 (paperback). YAC '95.

> The narrator Digger, who has made a career of digging graves, masterfully retells horror stories that will keep anyone glued to their seats while learning about werewolves, vampires, witches, and mummies.

A *Question of Time*

Fred Saberhagen. Tor. ISBN 0-312-851294. ISBN 0-812-52577-9 (paperback). YAC '94.

> Chapters from 1935 and 1991 alternate in this tale of suspense, romance, and time. Vampire Tyrell traps victims through a time slash in the Grand Canyon. In 1935 Jake, lured by a girl, fights futilely to escape. In 1991, Tyrell's widow hires detectives to find the niece missing at the canyon. This literary vampire can be compared with others.

Songsmith

Andre Norton and A.C. Crispin. Tor. ISBN 0-312-85123-5. ISBN 0-812-51107-7 (paperback). YAC '94.

> In this "Witch World" fantasy/adventure, Master Songsmith Eydrth encounters an evil witch determined to destroy male magic users and assume their power. With the help of Alon and his half-demon horse, Eydrth discovers her powers, deals with the witch, and searches for true love and a cure for her bespelled father.

Friendship and Romance

Buffalo Gal
Bill Wallace. Holiday House. ISBN 0-8234-0943-0. Minstrel (paperback). YAC '94.

> This turn-of-the-century adventure is full of suspense and romance between 16-year-old Amanda Guthridge and David Talltree, a half-Comanche ranch hand. In this fictionalized account of the Wild West, Amanda and her independent mother travel to Oklahoma and Texas to rescue a herd of buffalo.

Freak the Mighty
Rodman Philbrick. Scholastic. ISBN 0-590-47412-X. ISBN 0-590-47413-8 (paperback). YAC '95.

> Two outcasts form a strong friendship in this compelling novel. Max, a big, awkward, learning-disabled teenager, meets Kevin, who is small, brilliant, and sharp-tongued. They join to fight for good causes but when Kevin dies, Max is left with only memories to help him face the future. Teens can learn about triumph over imperfection, shame, and loss from this story.

Graveyard Moon

Carol Gorman. Avon. ISBN 0-380-76991-3 (paperback).
YAC '95.

> In this suspense story, a student who is new to Spencer Point
> High School undergoes an initiation at a graveyard. When
> the trick goes sour, she realizes her involvement is scarier
> than her worst nightmare.

A Little Bit Dead

Chap Reaver. Delacorte. ISBN 0-385-30801-9. Laurel
Leaf/Bantam Doubleday Dell. ISBN 0-440-21910-8 (paperback). YAC '94.

> This wonderful story set in the U.S. West of 1876 grapples
> with issues of loyalty, friendship, and compassion in a con-
> temporary way. The characters ring true as the lives of Native
> Americans and early settlers are described in authentic detail.

Nothing More, Nothing Less

Jane McFann. Avon. ISBN 0-380-76636-1 (paperback).
YAC '95.

> Mackenzie Paige Cameron thought falling in love was the
> key to a happy and a successful senior year in high school.
> The realistic experiences of high school life allow teenage
> readers to look at problems similar to their own and perhaps
> get a different perspective on them.

Please Don't Die

Lurlene McDaniel. Bantam. ISBN 0-553-56262-2. YAC '95.

> Four teenage girls, each with a life-threatening disease, spend
> the summer at Jenny's house and form a special friendship
> strong enough to endure the challenges that lie ahead.

The Wind Blows Backward
Mary Downing Hahn. Clarion. ISBN 0-395-62975-6.
YAC '95.

Although Spencer and Lauren were best friends in eighth grade, Spencer distances himself from her in high school, until he needs her friendship during their senior year. As these complex characters evolve, their friendship develops into love. High school readers will empathize as they discover the reasons for Spencer's moody, self-destructive side and witness the improvement of Lauren's self-esteem.

Health

Death Is Hard to Live With: Teenagers Talk About How They Cope with Loss
Janet Bode. Delacorte. ISBN 0-385-31041-2. Laurel Leaf. ISBN 0-440-21929-9 (paperback). YAC '95.

> This is a collection of real-life accounts of teenagers who have experienced the loss of a friend or loved one. The author explores ways of dealing with the shock, guilt, and emotional pain associated with death. In addition, specialists who deal with death every day provide statistics and thoughts on dying. Young adults can learn how to cope by reading about what worked for others.

Now I Lay Me Down to Sleep
Lurlene McDaniel. Bantam. ISBN 0-553-28897-0. YAC '93.

> Carrie Blake, 15, has suffered from leukemia for 3 years. With her disease in remission, she volunteers to help plan the hospital support group's annual picnic and meets Keith Gardner, who has Hodgkin's disease. She compares his warm, supportive family with her own divorced parents. When Keith's disease worsens, Carrie devotes her time to him and faces her own problems.

100 Questions and Answers About AIDS: A Guide for Young People

Michael Thomas Ford. New Discovery. ISBN 0-02-735424-5. YAC '94.

> Today's young adults are very interested in the topic of AIDS. This book addresses their questions in a well-organized fashion indexed by topic. Interviews with young people living with AIDS add a human interest touch.

Ryan White: My Own Story

Ryan White and Ann Marie Cunningham. Illustrated with photos. Dial. ISBN 0-8037-0977-3. YAC '93.

> The late Ryan White tells his story in the natural, engaging way in which he often reached out to others. He tells about contracting AIDS from an infected blood-clotting agent, being forced out of school in Kokomo, Indiana, and then moving to the welcoming community of Cicero. He talks most about his family and friends, a circle that became wider as Ryan spoke out about AIDS. Reader after reader called this book a "must read" for everyone.

Until Whatever

Martha Humphreys. Clarion. ISBN 0-395-58022-6. YAC '93.

> When the word spreads that Connie Tibbs has AIDS, she discovers how few friends she has in high school. Fortunately Karen, an acquaintance from the past, becomes a true friend during the final lonely days of Connie's life. Despite rejection from her peers, Karen gains empathy and discovers the value of friendship and commitment.

History:
Fiction and
Nonfiction

The Discoverers of America
Harold Faber. Scribner. ISBN 0-684-19217-9. YAC '94.

> This nonfiction book chronicles the discoverers of America,
> from the Native Americans who were believed to have
> crossed the Bering Strait after the last Ice Age through the
> Vikings and the major European explorers, and concludes
> with Bering's visit to Alaska and Cook's to Hawaii.

In My Father's House
Ann Rinaldi. Scholastic. ISBN 0-590-44730-0. ISBN 0-590-
44731-9 (paperback). YAC '95.

> Readers get a clear picture of what life was like for Southern
> families during the U.S. Civil War. This novel, based on the
> life of a man named Will McLean, is a sweeping, dramatic
> overview of the war and its moral dilemmas. The book is well
> researched and excellent for discussions.

Jacket painting ©1993 by Melissa Gallo. Reproduced by permission of Scholastic Hardcover.

Jericho's Journey

G. Clifton Wisler. Lodestar. ISBN 0-525-67428-4. YAC '95.

In 1852, 12-year-old Jericho's family makes a treacherous
covered-wagon journey from Tennessee to a new home in
Texas. Based on an actual diary, this book is a good choice for
units on westward expansion, family histories, or survival.

The Man from the Other Side
Uri Orlev. Translation by Hillel Halkin. Houghton Mifflin. ISBN 0-395-53808-4. YAC '93.

> The cruelty of Nazi oppression and the brutal hatred of many of his countrymen are brought home to 14-year-old Marek as he befriends Pan Jozek, a Jew on the run in German-occupied Warsaw in 1942. In his heroic efforts to help Jozek, Marek is swept into the Warsaw Ghetto uprising, as the outnumbered Jews use their pop guns against tanks. *The Other Victims, The Island on Bird Street,* and *The Diary of Anne Frank* can be read with this book to illuminate the dark side of humanity.

Navajo Code Talkers
Nathan Aaseng. Walker. ISBN 8027-8182-9. YAC '94.

> This is an interesting account of how Native American Navajos, using their unique language during World War II, served as code talkers, facilitating military operations in the Pacific. This book would appeal to those interested in learning more about Native Americans and World War II as well as army intelligence and cryptography.

Nothing to Fear
Jackie French Koller. Gulliver. ISBN 0-15-200544-7. YAC '93.

> This book was inspired by stories the author's mother told her about the hard times experienced during the Depression of the 1930s in the U.S. Danny Garvey's father must leave his newly immigrated family in New York City to look for work. In his father's absence, Danny becomes man of the house. This piece of historical fiction depicts a strong sense of family pride and the hardships families faced. The book would be a great supplement to an American studies course at either the junior or senior high level.

Red Sky at Morning

Andrea Wyman. Holiday House. ISBN 0-8234-0903-1.
YAC '93.

> Callie, 12, learns that life goes on in spite of deaths, diphtheria, caring for an aging grandfather and a farm, and the betrayal of a father. This book depicts daily life in the early 1900s, making it good supplementary historical reading. The relationship between Callie and her German immigrant grandfather make the book appropriate for intergenerational or multicultural units of study.

White Hare's Horses

Penina Keen Spinka. Atheneum. ISBN 0-689-31654-2.
YAC '93.

> In the Santa Monica Mountains in 16th-century California, Native American girl White Hare frees the horses used by an Aztec chieftain and his soldiers, thus foiling their attempts to enslave her people. The culture of White Hare's tribe is poetically presented, enhancing understanding of these little-known early Native Americans.

White Lilacs

Carolyn Meyer. Gulliver. ISBN 0-15-200641-9. ISBN 0-15-295876-2 (paperback). YAC '95.

> Based on an actual event from 1921 to 1922, this fictionalized story tells about the eviction of Freedomtown's African American residents to make way for a park in the center of town. This book can be compared to others that deal with injustice, prejudice, and individual bravery.

Witnesses to Freedom: Young People Who Fought for Civil Rights

Belinda Rochelle. Illustrated with photos. Lodestar. ISBN 0-525-67377-6. YAC '95.

> The profiles of young people in this book illustrate their personal struggles to fight for freedom in the 1950s and 1960s. They did not wait to become adults to take action against discrimination. After reading the book, students can identify ways to contribute in their own communities.

Year of Impossible Goodbyes

Sook Nyul Choi. Houghton Mifflin. ISBN 0-395-57419-6. Dell. ISBN 0-440-40759-1 (paperback). YAC '93.

> This book is based on the author's memories of her childhood under the Japanese and Russian occupation of North Korea during the 1940s. It portrays the horrors of the time and the human ability to overcome hardships. It makes history come alive and can be compared to other books about people in occupied lands.

Mystery and Crime

The Babysitter II
R.L. Stine. Scholastic. ISBN 0-590-44332-1. YAC '93.

In this sequel to *The Babysitter*, Jenny is terrorized by telephone calls from a whispery voice from the grave that repeats "Hi, Babes. I'm back." This horror mystery will appeal to the reluctant young adult reader. It can be discussed and compared with the many titles in this genre written by Stine and others.

The Christmas Killer
Patricia Windsor. Scholastic. ISBN 0-590-43311-3. Scholastic. ISBN 0-590-43310-5 (paperback). YAC '93.

A serial killer is murdering young women in tiny Bethboro, Connecticut, and Rose Potter's dreams have turned into nightmares as Nancy, the first victim, begins providing her with information about the other victims and the killer. Why has Nancy singled Rose out? Is Rose a witch? Will she unmask the murderer before she becomes his next victim? This Edgar Award-winning thriller is sure to appeal to reluctant readers.

Deathline
Barbara Steiner. Avon. ISBN 0-380-77066-0 (paperback).
YAC '95.

> Erica volunteers at Rapline, a phone-in counseling service for
> teens. When weird calls are matched to murders, Erica fears
> for her own life. Part of Avon's YA Horror series, this book is
> popular with young readers looking primarily for suspense
> rather than character development or writing style.

Nevernever
Will Shetterly. Harcourt Brace. ISBN 0-15-257022-5.
YAC '95.

> This fantasy, written in first person, is about the wolfboy
> Ron, now a teenager, who finds that growing up and surviv-
> ing as a mute wolf is difficult. Characters exist at different
> ages simultaneously, a mystery nicely explained at the end.

The Secret of Sanctuary Island
A.M. Monson. Lothrop. ISBN 0-688-10111-9. Beech Tree
Books. ISBN 0-688-11693-0 (paperback). YAC '93.

> While canoeing, seventh graders Todd and Kevin observe a
> burglary. This leads to a dangerous chase, uncovering a con
> game, and Todd's developing a better rapport with his step-
> mother. Students might compare this with other favorite
> mysteries or books that deal with stepparent relationships.

Surprise Party
Nicole Davidson. Avon. ISBN 0-380-76996-4 (paperback).
YAC '95.

> An intriguing stranger comes to town and Maureen finds her-
> self dangerously drawn to him. When she invites him to her
> party, the deadly game begins.

Terror at the Zoo

Peg Kehret. Cobblehill. ISBN 0-525-65083-0. Minstrel/Pocketbooks. ISBN 0-671-79394-2 (paperback). YAC '94.

> Ellen and Corey Streater get a joint birthday present, a pass to spend the night at Woodland Park Zoo. The night of the camp-out, their parents aren't home in time to take them. This excellent mystery book will keep you in constant suspense.

The Trouble with Lemons

Daniel Hayes. David R. Godine. ISBN 0-87923-825-9. Fawcett (paperback). YAC '93.

> When 13-year-old Tyler and his friend Lymie sneak out for a midnight swim, the last thing they expect to find is a dead body. The victim, a mildly retarded school janitor, was murdered. Tyler believes he knows who the murderer is and is determined to expose him. Hayes provides a great mystery and a thoroughly likeable and believable character who considers himself a "lemon" and faces familiar junior high problems of acceptance. Even hardcore reluctant readers will like this mystery.

Violence on America's Streets

Gene Brown. Millbrook. ISBN 1-56294-1550-0. ISBN 1-878841-95-5 (paperback). YAC '94.

> Gangs, violence, and gun control are just a few of the issues that Brown uses to hold his audience in this fact-filled book about crime and justice. Photos and a multitude of graphics clarify the readers' questions.

We All Fall Down

Robert Cormier. Delacorte. ISBN 0-385-30501-X. Dell. ISBN 0440-21556-0 (paperback). YAC '93.

> In this gritty, disturbing novel, Cormier charts the effects of an act of random violence on the Jerome family. Little does 16-year-old Jane Jerome realize that her life will become intertwined not only with one of the perpetrators of the crime, but also with the mystery person who witnessed it and now seeks vengeance.

Reprinted by permission of David R. Godine, Publisher, Inc.
Copyright ©1991 by Daniel Hayes. Jacket illustration by Fred Lynch.

Whatever Happened to Janie?

Caroline B. Cooney. Delacorte. ISBN 0-385-31035-8. Laurel
Leaf. ISBN 0-440-21924-8 (paperback). YAC '95.

> In this sequel to *The Face on the Milk Carton*, the author explores family ties, loyalty, adolescent identity, and self-esteem. Taking the seeds of its plot from kidnapping and adoption stories found in today's newspapers, this fictionalized account will interest even the most reluctant reader.

Nature and Ecology

The Ancient One
T.A. Barron. Philomel. ISBN 0-399-21899-8. YAC '94.

> Kate, a 13-year-old visiting her aunt in Oregon, tries to save the redwood trees from loggers in Lost Crater, a place where an Indian tribe vanished centuries ago. The book lends itself to a study of environmentalists versus loggers.

Lost Civilizations
Dorothy Hoobler and Thomas Hoobler. Walker. ISBN 0-8027-8152-7. YAC '94.

> This book presents unanswered questions about the mysteries of Stonehenge, Atlantis, Easter Island, and Pre-Columbian and Minoan artifacts. To dispel fantasies, the authors provide documentation for most of the remarkable phenomena while acknowledging that gaps in knowledge await further scientific investigation.

Our Endangered Planet: Population Growth

Suzanne Winckler and Mary M. Rodgers. Illustrated with photographs. Lerner. ISBN 0-8225-2502-X. YAC '93.

Part of the *Our Endangered Planet* series and written primarily for 8- to 12-year-olds, this book interests readers of all ages. Many experts assert that most of the world's environmental troubles are due to human overpopulation. *Population Growth*, printed on recycled paper, explores its causes and effects and proposes some solutions. One reader responded: "I liked the parts about signs of global stress, about the ozone layer, and

the changing climate. After reading this, I went out and recycled some old newspapers."

Predator!

Bruce Brooks. Illustrated with photos. Farrar, Straus &
Giroux. ISBN 0-374-36111-8. YAC '93.

Winner of a Newbery Honor for his fiction writing, Bruce
Brooks uses the same informal, engaging style in this nonfiction text. He captures the drama of animals' struggle to eat
and to escape being eaten. Brooks uses scientific terminology
and in-depth factual information about prey and predator be-
havior and includes colorful photos, a useful glossary, and an
index. The book ends with a warning about human interfer-
ence with the food chain.

Personal Growth

The Atonement of Mindy Wise
Marilyn Kaye. Gulliver. ISBN 0-15-200402-5. YAC '93.

When Mindy was 13-years old, her family moved and she was determined to become part of the in crowd. In doing so, she committed many sins: lying, disobeying, gossiping, cheating, betraying, and snubbing. The story opens with Mindy recalling her sins of the past year while sitting through a Yom Kippur service. The book is subtle in its moralizing and does not turn readers off. Junior high students are able to relate to Mindy's sins and reflect on them from a distance.

Cages
Peg Kehret. Cobblehill. ISBN 0-525-65062-8. YAC '93.

Kit, a ninth grader, deals poorly with school frustrations, an alcoholic stepfather, and an ineffectual mother. She is caught shoplifting and chooses community service at the Society for the Prevention of Cruelty to Animals as her punishment. An elderly volunteer gives her insight that develops Kit's inner strength. Adolescents will relate to Kit's feelings of helplessness, and teachers will find good examples of cause and effect as well as a springboard for teaching effective problem-solving skills.

Colt

Nancy Springer. Dial. ISBN 0-8037-1022-4. YAC '93.

> Colt, handicapped by spina bifida, sheds his dependence as he learns to ride horses. This is a fine novel to use in a unit on people with handicaps or overcoming difficult odds.

Crazy Lady!

Jane Leslie Conly. Harper Trophy. ISBN 0-06-440571-0 (paperback). YAC '95.

> In this heart-tugging story, teenage Vernon and his friends tease a neighborhood alcoholic and her retarded son. As he gets to know this family better, Vernon comes to terms with the death of his mother, a father who is busy with family responsibilities, and poor performance at school. The book teaches compassion and discovering one's strength in the face of loss and adversity.

Crosses

Shelley Stoehr. Delacorte. ISBN 0-385-30451-X. Laurel Leaf. ISBN 0440-21561-7 (paperback). YAC '93.

> Nancy's first-person narrative of her troubled adolescence is filled with expletives, punk dress, shoplifting, sex, drugs, alcohol, and the physical pain and thrill of "cuttings," which seem to assuage her emotional turmoil. Stoehr's account is honest and hard hitting. Several parents and teens read the book together and responded positively to its implicit warnings about drug and alcohol abuse. One reader called it "the Go Ask Alice of the 90s."

Emily Good as Gold

Susan Goldman Rubin. Browndeer Press, Harcourt Brace. ISBN 0-15-276632-4. Browndeer Press. ISBN 0-15-276633-2 (paperback). YAC '95.

> A special teenager is sympathetically portrayed. Thirteen years old and developmentally disabled, pretty Emily Gold just wants to be like other girls her age. All teenage girls will be able to relate to her problems.

Jacket art ©1993 by Elena Pavlov from Crazy Lady! *by Jane Leslie Conly.*

Finding My Voice

Marie G. Lee. Houghton Mifflin. ISBN 0-395-62134-8. YAC '94.

> Ellen, a Korean American teenager, struggles to define her identity when living in two cultures. This book can be discussed and compared with other multiethnic titles portraying the tensions within minority characters. This realistic novel also includes many adolescent experiences with which students can identify.

Four of a Kind
Patti Sherlock. Holiday House. ISBN 0-8234-0913-9.
YAC '93.

Andy dreams of training two colts for a pulling contest. First
he must convince Grandpa to let him buy the horses and
help train them. Themes in this story include family relationships, accepting responsibility, and pursuing dreams. Students
could translate the settings and episodes into artwork, short
stories capturing Grandpa's background, and personal reflections comparing Andy's growth and ambitions with their
own. The descriptions make this a good source for urban students who are limited in their knowledge of rural experiences.

Love, David
Dianne Case. Illustrated by Dan Andreasen. Lodestar. ISBN
0-525-67350-4. YAC '93.

Growing up labeled as colored in South Africa is difficult for
Anna, especially when her beloved brother David becomes
involved in selling drugs to escape dire poverty. This realistic
picture of life in apartheid South Africa can be used in middle school with other novels such as *Journey to Jo'burg* and
Chain of Fire to better understand discrimination in that
country.

Lucy Peale
Colby Rodowsky. Farrar, Straus & Giroux. ISBN 0-374-
36381-1. Aerial Fiction/FSG. ISBN 0-374-44659-8 (paperback). YAC '94.

After forced sex, Lucy runs away from home and her evange-
list father, rather than declare her sinfulness at a prayer meeting. A young man finds her homeless, pregnant, and hungry.
While reading this realistic fiction novel, students can re-
spond in reading logs and discuss issues in small groups.

Mel
Liz Berry. Viking. ISBN 0-670-83925-6. YAC '93.

Self-reliance and care and concern for others are the dual themes of this novel. Seventeen-year-old Mel Calder struggles to survive a London slum and the loss of her mother to mental illness. After a failed suicide attempt, she takes charge of her life and surroundings. Artistic expression, political activism, the development of entrepreneurial talents, and a stormy relationship with a rock star follow.

Weeping Willow
Ruth White. Farrar, Straus & Giroux. ISBN 0-374-38255-7. Aerial Fiction/FSG. ISBN 0-374-48380-2 (paperback). YAC '94.

In this coming-of-age novel, Tiny Lambert develops from a shy, friendless high school freshman to a popular, confident senior. Set in the 1950s in rural Virginia, the story traces Tiny's efforts to overcome family difficulties. This realistic novel could become a springboard for reflective writing and discussion on personal relationships between teens and adults.

Where Do I Go from Here?
Valerie Wilson Wesley. Scholastic. ISBN 0-590-45606-7. ISBN 0-590-45607-5 (paperback). YAC '95.

Through the experiences of Nia, one of only two African American scholarship students at an exclusive boarding school, the reader learns about being an outsider, the effect of everyday decisions, and the importance of educational opportunities. This realistic story is positive but not preachy. Characters and dialogue keep readers' interest.

Science Fiction

Jumper
Steven Gould. Tor. ISBN 0-812-52237-0 (paperback). YAC '94.

An inordinately good science fiction story that makes teleportation seem not only believable, but practical, Jumper will appeal to any readers who want a fast-paced adventure story with lots of action and a likable main character. Seventeen-year-old Davy initially "jumps" to escape abuse but then finds it convenient for dating, financial support, revenge, capturing terrorists, and evading government agents tracking him.

Keeper of the Universe
Louise Lawrence. Clarion. ISBN 0-395-64340-6. YAC '94.

When transported to another galaxy, Christopher slowly comes to the anguished conclusion that acting according to one's conscience is the ultimate meaning of humanity. He has to decide whether guaranteeing peace based on mind control methods is worth it to save Earth from total destruction. This novel lends itself to discussions of moral responsibility and freedom of choice.

Sports

Backfield Package
Thomas J. Dygard. Morrow. ISBN 0-688-11471-7. YAC '94.
> Four football players formed a close friendship as they played on their high school team. They agreed to stick together, attend the same college, and play football for another four years. This teenage sports fiction novel can be compared with other books focusing on suspense, decision making, and choices.

Blowing Bubbles with the Enemy
Alison Jackson. Dutton. ISBN 0-525-450564. YAC '95.
> When Bobby Lorimar, a talented sixth grade female basketball player, attempts to try out for the middle school boys' team, she encounters prejudice and harassment and jeopardizes a budding friendship with one of the players. Jackson's honest discussion of the issue and her satisfying resolution appeal even to older readers.

Deion Sanders: Prime Time Player
Stew Thornley. Illustrated with photos. Lerner. ISBN 0-8225-0523-1. First Avenue North. ISBN 0-8225-9648-2 (paperback). YAC '95.
> This is a rapid-fire account of Deion Sanders' athletic success playing two professional sports at the same time. This illustrated biography for young adolescents presents an athlete who, despite his flamboyant appearance and wise-cracking comments, is worthy of young readers' admiration for his activities on and off the field.

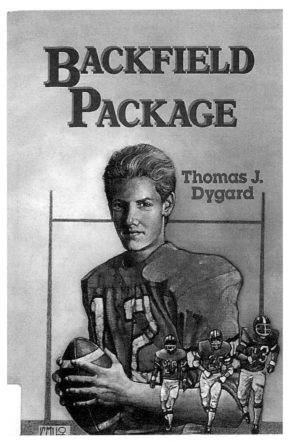

Jackie Robinson

Manfred Weidhorn. Illustrated with photos. Atheneum.
ISBN 0-689-31644-5. YAC '95.

> The era and the man are fondly recalled in this hard-hitting
> biography. Pulling no punches, it tells what prepared Jackie
> Robinson to break the color barrier in professional sports and
> his evolution as a spokesman for African Americans. The
> book is useful for social studies classes and as an exciting
> biography of one of baseball's Hall of Fame players.

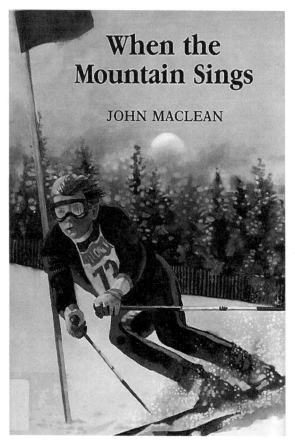

When the
Mountain Sings

JOHN MACLEAN

When the Mountain Sings

John MacLean. Houghton Mifflin. ISBN 0-395-59917-2. YAC '94.

Ski enthusiasts will particularly enjoy MacLean's story about 13-year-old Sam's first season of competitive skiing. From his first meet to his final race in the state competition, readers will share his fear of failure on the slopes, his budding competitiveness, and his mixed feelings at skiing in the state final as an alternate because a teammate was injured.

Author Index

Title Index

51

Also available from IRA...

If children read books they like, they will like to read. Here are three lists of books that have been tested and endorsed by the experts— real kids, teens, and teachers. These lists are a wonderful source for parents, teachers, and young readers alike. Children's Choices is a listing of new children's books that school children from across the U.S. chose as their favorites. Young Adults' Choices includes books selected by young adult readers as the ones they consider the most enjoyable and informative. Teachers' Choices identifies the new trade books for children and adolescents that classroom teachers consider to be exceptional in curriculum use. All lists include annotations and bibliographic information.

Booklists are available at the following rates:

10 copies	$6.00
100 copies	$45.00
500 copies	$170.00

To order your copies of Children's Choices, Young Adults' Choices, or Teachers' Choices, call 1-800-336-READ, ext. 266 (outside North America call 302-731-1600, ext. 266).

Children's Choices	No. 386-828
Young Adults' Choices	No. 387-828
Teachers' Choices	No. 388-828